MOTORHOME CUISINE PRESENTS:

42 ESSENTIAL RECIPES
FOR YOUR MOTORHOME/RV

CHRISTOPHER REX LLOYD

INTRODUCTION

Open up and welcome aboard *42 Essential Recipes for Your Motorhome/RV*, a recipe book designed for the spontaneous, adventurous, and free-spirited soul that all motorhome/RV owners possess. This collection is packed with tips and ideas that will save you time and money, offers you the confidence and knowledge to safely operate all of the amenities that your motorhome/RV has to offer, and uses ingredients that will provide you with the energy needed to tack on those miles, see the sights, and hike the hikes. Any item in this book can be executed in a rest area, parking lot, or a campground. Wherever you are, this book will provide you with the ability to create a gourmet meal that will keep you healthy, energetic, and nourished while traveling, without consuming too much of your valuable time.

Making this book part of your routine can save you a substantial amount of time, and the trouble of having to eat out. It can be frustrating having to drive through town, find a parking spot—and then the whole dining experience can last up to an hour. Making a habit of eating out can be costly, and can affect your travel time drastically. Everything in this book can be done in less than 30 minutes, and that includes the clean-up time. By using only one pot or pan, you will avoid wasting water and time on a massive pile of dishes. While most of these recipes call for, on average, about eight dollars' worth of ingredients, the time that you save by using this book is priceless.

Quick, simple, and healthy is the name of the game when providing meals for your crew on the road. Eventually, Easy Mac, Hamburger Helper, and Rice-A-Roni will wear out their welcome in your home on the road. When that happens, this book will give you the upper hand in the motorhome/RV dining experience. Nothing compares to the feeling of fulfillment created by making your own meal. To make sure your vacation or even your day is fulfilled, use these essential recipes. Whether you're going east, west, north, or south, be sure to pack *42 Essential Recipes for Your Motorhome/RV*.

SAFETY FIRST

One of the most dangerous and feared aspects of a motorhome/RV is the propane system, and it's for a good reason. Leaking propane in your motorhome can cause carbon monoxide poisoning, which can lead to death by asphyxiation or even an explosion. Propane should be your number-one priority when traveling. Always knowing when your tank is open or closed could be the difference between life and death. Simple procedures will help you maintain a safe environment when using the amenities that the propane supplies. Be sure to thoroughly read and comprehend every user manual of every appliance that uses propane before even touching your main propane supply tank.

Lighting a pilot light should be done with extreme caution and the knowledge of what to expect and how to operate that specific appliance. A wise man is scared when lighting a pilot light, simply because he knows the danger and threat that leaking propane has to offer. I've found my comfort level has increased since I created certain procedures to follow when operating an appliance that uses propane. For example: When I'm done using a burner or an oven, I will always turn off the main propane tank first, allowing all of the propane to burn away, leaving all of the propane lines empty. After the propane has emptied out of the hoses, I then proceed to turn off the appliance. This ensures there is no stored propane in your living space that could potentially be hazardous.

Once you have an understanding of every appliance and now have the confidence to operate all of your amenities, it's a good idea to know safe food handling. Nothing can ruin a trip quite like food poisoning. An important item to carry on board is a meat thermometer, and then knowing the proper food temperatures is the next step to avoid food poisoning. Chicken and pork can be deadly if not prepared correctly. Always make sure to cook your chicken and pork to at least 160° Fahrenheit. For beef, it's a good idea to cook to at least 150° Fahrenheit, which is a little over medium. The source and cut of the meat determines how it should be cooked. If it's fresh beef straight from the source, then you could get away with 135° to 145° Fahrenheit.

The same goes for fish: whether it's fresh or frozen determines what temperature it needs to be cooked to. Coming from a landlocked state, I cook all my fish to 150° Fahrenheit.

Improperly cooked food isn't the only way to obtain food poisoning. Cross-contamination can also cause a food-borne illness. When handling any kind of meat, fish, or poultry, always wash any utensil that has come into contact with those items. When washing utensils, always follow the proper procedure of making sure all soap has been rinsed off and has had ample time to dry. Consuming dish soap can easily fill up your septic tank. So let this knowledge keep you safe and healthy on the road.

HEALTHY LIVING

Eating healthy has become a concern in our country, and for good reason. According to the American diabetes association Almost 10% of Americans live with diabetes, and the C.D.C. says that one in three adults are victims of high-blood pressure. Three out of every four men are considered to be overweight or obese stated the N.I.H. All of these conditions have drastically changed the lives of the people diagnosed with them. While this book will not solve those problems, it will provide tips and recommendations to help you take the steps necessary to pursue and live a healthy lifestyle. A healthy camper is a happy camper, and a happy camper is the camper we all want to be.

Counting carbs, sugars, and fats is essential to living a healthy lifestyle. Getting the proper nutrition and the correct amount of servings from certain food groups is just as important. Preparing your own meals helps you keep track of the amount of servings you receive from each food group. I have used certain ingredients in these recipes with healthy attributes for your diet, such as foods that are high in fiber and protein to supply you with the energy and nutrition needed to keep you active, awake, and enthusiastic about your long-awaited adventures. Some ingredients, like coconut oil, are used in this book simply because they are more beneficial than others. While olive oil isn't bad for you, it just isn't as beneficial for the active body.

The fulfillment of preparing your own meal is unmatched by anything that comes from a box or restaurant. While eating meals from boxes may be convenient and easy, making a habit of it will affect your health in the long run due to their high amounts of sodium. Cooking can be very intimidating, but, like all pursuits in life, it can be perfected with time, practice, and patience. Eventually, preparing and cooking your own meals will become an instinct, and you will gain the confidence to explore and try new recipes. Before you know it, you will be more than happy to cook dinner for your posse.

PRE-COOKING

Planning out a trip in advance is a good way to manage your travel time, and to know how much leisure time you will have available. While a motorhome/RVer's main priority is leisure, a few preparation tips will allow you to enjoy all of your well-deserved time to relax and enjoy your travels. Pre-planning your meals will save you the hassle of driving through town and finding a parking spot, all while wasting gas and time. To avoid all of that, you have two options. You can eat food from a factory that comes out of a box, or you can create a meal that will provide you with the protein and nutrients needed to give you the energy for the miles that lie ahead.

Certain recipes in this book call for ingredients that are already cooked. One of the pre-cooked items is pasta. Cooking pasta in advance can save you at least 15 minutes, about a gallon of water, and a little propane. Generally when cooking pasta in advance, you want to cook it al dente (a little undercooked), and always be sure to cool it to room temperature before storing it. Once the pasta has cooled, pour a little canola oil over it and mix thoroughly. This prevents the pasta from sticking together and making it very hard to work with. For every box of pasta you cook, use about ¼ cup of oil. Always be sure to store cooked pasta in the fridge, where it can last up to a week; I've personally seen it last two weeks.

Another pre-cooked ingredient in this book is quinoa (keen-wah). Quinoa may not be everyone's favorite, but its nutritional value is too beneficial to leave out. Quinoa, the superfood, is the only grain that contains all 9 amino acids and is considered a complete protein plant food. It's packed with iron, fiber, and protein to provide you with the much-needed energy for traveling. While shopping at a grocery store, you may see that there are multiple types of quinoa. There's a dark-colored quinoa, a white quinoa, and a medley. While they all take the same amount of time to cook, the difference is in the texture of the grain when it's done. The white quinoa tends to cook up to a fluffy, soft, tender texture, while the dark-colored quinoa (black and red) tends to cook up with more of a crunchy texture. I personally prefer the medley colored. Keep in mind that most of it is never factory washed. Always be sure to rinse it thoroughly before cooking it. You also may want to consider whether you would prefer a sweet taste or a savory taste. For a sweet taste, cook the quinoa in some type of juice, such as orange, apple, grapefruit, or my favorite, pomegranate juice. For a savory taste, you can use a chicken or vegetable stock. Always remember to let the quinoa cool to room temperature before storing it in your fridge. Also, always store your cooked quinoa in a fridge. The shelf life can be from a week to two weeks. If you find yourself with an excess of cooked quinoa, it can go great in your eggs for the omelets or frittata, and will provide you with a little more protein.

Using bottled citrus juice and liquid eggs will not only save you time, but also save you from having unwanted waste cluttering up your space. Citrus juice is used multiple times in this book, and it will be well worth the sacrifice to use pre-squeezed citrus juice rather than squeezing it fresh. Most pre-packaged citrus juices are equivalent to about 6 limes or lemons. Using pre-squeezed citrus will prevent you from attracting unwanted flies, aromas, and trash, while providing you with more leisure time and storage space. Using liquid eggs will also help conserve time, space, and waste. They save the time of cracking eggshells, they save the room in the trash that the broken shells would take up, and they save you the mess of having to dirty a dish just to scramble eggs. Those three traits are a top priority while traveling and are the reason they are used in this book.

Every second counts while traveling, and wasted time adds up to an unfulfilled vacation. Although cooking inside your camper can be a little unnerving and intimidating at first, just keep practicing and cooking; eventually, you'll feel like you're on the Food Network, cooking up elegant meals for the family. It will be well worth your time and money to learn the ins and outs of your kitchen and all of the amenities that your motorhome/RV has to offer. After all, that is why we all own one.

Items Needed

- Large saucepot
- Large sauté pan
- Large cast-iron pan
- Egg pan
- Small non-stick pan
- Baking sheet
- Cutting board
- Chef knife
- Strainer
- Can opener
- Meat thermometer
- Wooden spoon
- Measuring device
- Large mixing bowl
- Rubber and metal spatulas
- Whisk
- Vegetable peeler
- Non-stick cooking spray
- 1-gallon ziplock bag
- Utensils to enjoy your delicious creations
- Proper sanitation to prevent food-borne illnesses
- Appetite
- Wine-bottle corkscrew
- Wine glasses

TABLE OF CONTENTS

BREAKFAST
RECIPES

BERRIES AND CREAM CRÊPE

The art of making a crêpe is a skill that's perfected with practice, patience, and time. Similar to the omelet, it is a step-by-step process that takes a certain finesse learned through trial and error. It is a culinary skill that will be worth your while to learn, perfect, and enjoy. The recipe that I've provided you is typically a breakfast crêpe, but if you've become inspired by your new skill, feel free to expand out to savory or dessert crêpes. On average, this recipe produces about 12 crêpes, and unused batter can be refrigerated for another day or meal.

BATTER INGREDIENTS

- 1 cup all-purpose flour
- 1 ½ cup milk
- ½ cup liquid eggs
- 1 teaspoon vegetable oil
- ¼ teaspoon salt
- Non-stick cooking spray

Combine all of the ingredients (except the cooking spray) in a bowl and mix well. Heat a small non-stick pan over medium heat until the pan is hot. Once pan is hot, generously coat the pan with cooking spray. Pour ¼ cup of batter into one side of your pan, and tilt it in a circular motion so that the batter spreads evenly and covers the entire bottom of your pan. Return the pan to the heat and cook until the edges of the batter start to brown. Then, gently pry the batter off of the pan, flip, and continue cooking for 30 to 45 seconds. To remove, flip the pan onto a paper towel, and then repeat until all batter has been used.

FILLING INGREDIENTS

There are many different fillings that you can put into a crêpe. If you are on a tight time schedule, feel free to use fresh raw berries. If time is not an issue, then I highly recommend the warm filling recipe provided, because it softens up the crêpes and adds a little more flavor to your plate.

- 32 ounces of frozen berries (your choice)
- 6.5 ounce-can low-fat Redi-Whip
- 1 tablespoon vanilla extract
- 1 tablespoon ground cinnamon

In a large pot, combine the berries, vanilla, and cinnamon, and let cook over medium heat until all of the berries have thawed and softened. Lay a crêpe out onto a plate and spray a line of Redi-Whip cream directly down the center of the crepe. Then spoon 2 to 3 ounces of berries onto the whipped cream. Gently roll each side of the crêpe over the filling and then serve.

Prep time: 10 minutes
Cook time: 20 minutes
Cleanup time: 8 minutes

SERVES 2 TO 3

Items needed: mixing bowl, whisk, measuring device, small non-stick pan, and large pot

13

CAST-IRON FRITTATA

A frittata is a quiche without the crust. This is a perfect option if you are traveling with a group of at least four people. Feel free to add your own ingredients you may have lying around that need to be used. Pretty much anything that you would eat with eggs can be added to a frittata. Nothing compares to camping with friends and waking them up with a steaming-hot, straight-out-of-the-oven breakfast for all of you to enjoy.

- 3 ½ cups of liquid eggs
- ½ cup canned sweet corn, drained
- ½ cup canned black beans, drained
- 1 jalapeño, diced small
- 1 small red pepper, diced
- 2 tablespoons cilantro, roughly chopped
- 1 teaspoon salt
- 1 teaspoon pepper
- Non-stick cooking spray

Preheat oven to 350°F and coat your cast-iron pan with non-stick cooking spray. Pour your liquid eggs into the pan and place it in the heated oven. Let cook for 10 minutes. Pull the pan out of the oven and evenly distribute the rest of the ingredients over the top of your half-cooked eggs, then place back into the oven. Finish cooking another 20 minutes. Check to see if the eggs are fully cooked by inserting a toothpick into the center, and if it comes out dry then it's ready. If there is moisture or uncooked egg on the toothpick, place the pan back in the oven and finish cooking for another 5 minutes. When pulling the pan out of the oven, place the pan on a hot pad to prevent your countertop from melting. Let cool for 10 minutes.

Prep time: 5 minutes

Cook time: 25 to 35 minutes

Cleanup time: 5 minutes

SERVES 4 TO 6

Items needed: cutting board, chef knife, measuring device, and cast-iron pan

BISCUITS AND GRAVY

For the biscuit in this recipe, I choose to use packaged biscuits because it requires you to heat your oven to 350°F, instead of cooking from scratch, which takes an oven temperature of at least 425°F. I personally enjoy the Pillsbury biscuit myself, but you can choose your favorite for this recipe. I use chorizo in the gravy because it has the most grease and flavor, which gets absorbed by the flour and gives your gravy a stronger taste without needing too many ingredients. Breakfast sausage works just as well, but, it doesn't have the spicy flavor that chorizo has.

- 1 16-ounce package of biscuits (your choice)
- 1 10-ounce package of chorizo or breakfast sausage
- ¼ cup of flour
- 2 ½ cups milk
- Pinch of salt and pepper

Cook the biscuits according to the package instructions. In a saucepot, cook the meat over medium heat until it is thoroughly cooked (about 8 minutes). Gradually stir in the flour with a whisk until grease and flour are well incorporated. Slowly pour in the milk while stirring, and bring to a boil. Turn heat down to low and let boil for about 5 minutes, while stirring, until sauce has thickened. Once sauce is thickened, pour over biscuits and enjoy.

Prep time: 5 minutes

Cook time: 20 minutes

Cleanup time: 5 minutes

SERVES 4

Items needed: saucepot, baking sheet, whisk, and measuring device

FRENCH TOAST

French toast can be done several different ways. The recipe provided in this book is the quickest and easiest that I know of. When making French toast in your motorhome/RV, you want to keep in mind that everything you're working with is smaller, from the flame to the pan. One thing that's helped me to make consistent French toast is to use the smallest bread I can find. Most stores have very small loaves of sliced white bread.

- 8 slices of small white bread
- ½ cup liquid eggs
- ½ cup milk
- 1 tablespoon vanilla extract
- 1 tablespoon cinnamon
- Non-stick cooking spray
- favorite brand of syrup

Mix the eggs, milk, cinnamon, and vanilla extract in a bowl, and heat your cast-iron pan over medium heat. Generously coat your pan with non-stick cooking spray. To avoid making a mess, pour a small portion of egg mixture onto a plate, take a slice of bread, and quickly dip each side of the bread into the batter and place into the pan in an organized manner, so you can fit multiple slices in the pan at a time (usually 4 slices at a time). Let the bread cook on each side for 1 ½ minutes. Repeat until all the batter is gone. Serve with your favorite syrup.

Prep time: 5 minutes

Cook time: 10 minutes

Cleanup time: 6 minutes

Items needed: cast-iron pan, metal spatula, mixing bowl, measuring device, and deep plate

RUSSET POTATO HASH

Cooking a proper hash is about adding the right ingredients at the right time and making sure your pan doesn't get too hot and burn the garlic. Don't be intimidated if it doesn't come out to your standard of quality the first time. It will take a couple times before you master the hash. But once you do, it will all be worth it. What's nice about the hash is that it is a well-rounded, nutritious meal that will benefit you on your long-awaited travels.

- ⮑ 2 large russet potatoes, cubed small
- ⮑ 1 small white onion, diced small
- ⮑ 1 red bell pepper, diced small
- ⮑ 2 cloves garlic, chopped fine
- ⮑ 2 tablespoons parsley, chopped
- ⮑ 1 tablespoon salt
- ⮑ 1/2 tablespoon black pepper
- ⮑ 2 tablespoons canola oil
- ⮑ 2 eggs

Heat your cast-iron pan over high heat, and then add canola oil. Once the oil in your pan starts to smoke, place the potatoes in the pan so each cube is touching the surface. Add the salt and pepper on top of the potatoes and let cook for about 3 minutes (don't stir the potatoes; let them sit for 3 minutes). You're going to be looking for the potato to form a golden-brown color on the side that's touching the pan (check by taking out one potato to see if this color has formed). Once the side of the potato has reached this color and texture, go ahead and stir all of the potatoes until you can see color on every potato cube. Once stirred, turn the heat down to medium, and add the red bell pepper and onion. Let the veggies sit on top of the potatoes for 2 minutes, then add your garlic and parsley and stir everything together. Continue cooking for 1 minute, then remove from heat and portion out onto plates. Heat your egg pan and break 1 egg into the non-stick pan. Cook egg to desired texture, place on top of your plated potatoes, and repeat with your second egg.

Prep time: 10 minutes

Cook time: 12 minutes

Cleanup time: 5 minutes

SERVES 2

Items needed: cast-iron pan, egg pan, chef knife, measuring device, and cutting board

THE OMELET

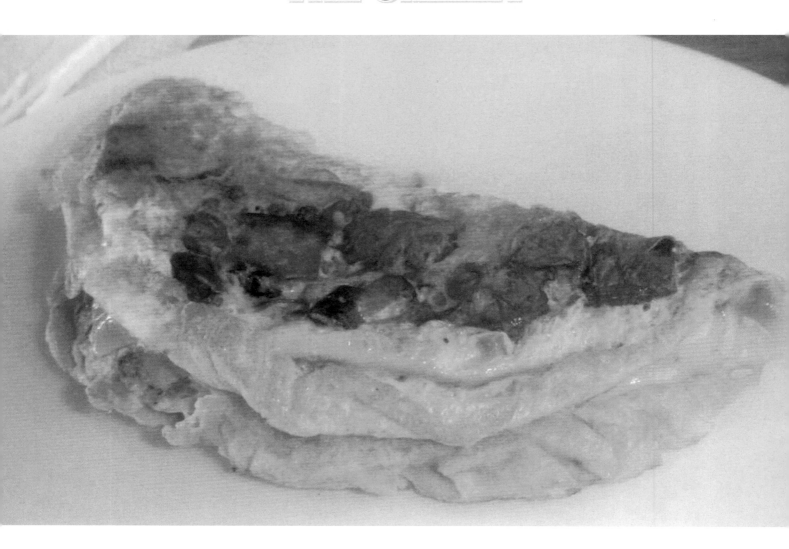

An omelet can be made two different ways. You can cook the ingredients in the egg pan, pour the raw eggs over the ingredients, and then cook the eggs. Or, the second way to enjoy the omelet is to cook the ingredients and set them aside, cook and flip the eggs, place the ingredients on top of the cooked eggs, and then fold the egg over them. Here are a few classic recipes that are foolproof and have earned their place in the timeless-omelet recipe list.

MUSHROOM, SPINACH, AND SWISS OMELET

Eating spinach always reminds me of watching Popeye when I was a kid, when he would crack open the can, chug the spinach, and grow muscles. It was very inspiring for me to consume spinach. You're going to want to make sure your mushrooms are thinly sliced, or even diced, so that they cook fast and all the way through. If you only have access to regular spinach, you can just use a knife to chop it.

- 1 ½ cups liquid eggs
- 6 portabella mushrooms, sliced thin
- 1 handful baby spinach
- 1 cup of shredded Swiss cheese
- 2 tablespoons coconut oil
- Pinch of salt and pepper

In your egg pan, heat 1 tablespoon of coconut oil over medium heat. Place half of the thinly sliced mushrooms into the pan and cook for about 1 minute, stirring frequently. Once the mushrooms are cooked, add half of the handful of baby spinach and cook for about 30 seconds. Once spinach starts to wilt, pour ¾ cup of eggs into the pan and cook until the eggs have set. Once set, fan the omelet by prying up one side of the egg with a rubber spatula, allowing excess liquid egg to run under the spatula and cook; repeat on the other side of the pan. Once cooked, flip the eggs as a whole and place Swiss cheese on top of the cooked eggs. Plate by sliding the half of cooked eggs onto the plate, and fold the other half of eggs over the top. Repeat with the remaining ingredients.

Prep time: 5 minutes

Cook time: 12 minutes

Cleanup time: 5 minutes

Items needed: egg pan, cutting board, chef knife, rubber spatula, and measuring device

SOUTHWEST OMELET

I love to enjoy this omelet while traveling through the desert; it really captures that Southwest feel. It can be a little spicy, and can also get a little runny if you don't strain your beans and corn well enough. Make sure to allow ample time for your vegetables to drain.

- 1 ½ cups liquid eggs
- ½ cup canned corn kernels, strained
- ½ cup canned black beans, strained
- 1 jalapeño, diced
- 1 Roma tomato, diced
- 2 tablespoons cilantro, chopped
- 1 cup shredded cheddar cheese
- 2 tablespoons coconut oil

In your egg pan, warm 1 tablespoon of coconut oil over medium heat. Pour ¾ cup of liquid egg into the pan and then place half of the corn, black beans, diced Roma tomato, and jalapeño evenly on top of the raw eggs. Let the eggs cook until the base has set and is firm. Once set, fan the omelet by prying up one side of the egg with a rubber spatula, allowing excess liquid egg to run under the spatula and cook; repeat on the other side of the pan. Once most of the liquid has set, flip the eggs as a whole, place half of the cheddar and cilantro on top of the cooked eggs, and cook for 1 minute. Plate by sliding the half of cooked eggs onto the plate, and fold the other half of eggs over the top. Repeat with the remaining ingredients.

Prep time: 10 minutes   Cook time: 15 minutes

Cleanup time: 6 minutes

SERVES 2

Items needed: egg pan, rubber spatula, measuring device, chef knife, cutting board, and strainer

THE DENVER OMELET

One of the most famous omelets to date, hands down, is the Denver omelet.

- 1 ½ cups liquid eggs
- 1 small red bell pepper, diced
- 1 small red onion, diced
- 6 thin slices of ham
- 1 cup shredded cheddar cheese
- 2 tablespoons coconut oil

In your egg pan, warm 1 tablespoon of coconut oil over medium heat and place half of the onion and red pepper into the pan. When they appear translucent, pour ¾ cup of liquid eggs over the top of the ingredients and cook until the bottom of the eggs have set. Once set, fan the omelet by prying up one side of the egg with a rubber spatula, allowing excess liquid egg to run under the spatula and cook; repeat on the other side of the pan. Once the bottom of the eggs appears to be cooked, flip the eggs as a whole and let cook for 1 minute. Disperse ½ cup of cheese on top of the cooked eggs. Then, on top of the cheese, lay 3 thin slices of ham. Plate by sliding the half of cooked eggs onto the plate, and fold the other half of eggs over the top. Repeat with the remaining ingredients.

Prep time: 8 minutes

Cook time: 15 minutes

Cleanup time: 5 minutes

SERVES 2

Items needed: measuring device, egg pan, chef knife, cutting board, and rubber spatula

BAKED EGGS WITH VEGGIES

Although the title says Baked Eggs, there's no need to worry about preheating the oven or even using it. All you need is your large sauté pan and a lid; the baking process happens when you cover your pan with the lid. This recipe is great because it provides you with plenty of nutrition and the joy of a nice runny yolk (if that's your preference). For a solid egg yolk, cook for 2 extra minutes.

- 4 eggs
- 8 baby bella mushrooms, thin sliced
- ½ small red onion, chopped
- 2 handfuls of spinach
- 1 tablespoon chopped garlic
- 2 Roma tomatoes, chopped
- 1 tablespoon coconut oil
- 1 teaspoon salt
- 2 tablespoons water

In your sauté pan, melt the coconut oil over medium heat. Add your mushrooms and let cook for about 2 minutes. Add garlic and onion and let cook for 2 more minutes. Then add your diced tomato, handfuls of spinach, and salt, and let cook for 1 more minute. After all ingredients are cooked, turn heat to low. Make 4 little pockets; these will be the supports for your eggs. Carefully crack the eggs into the formed pockets. If you don't feel comfortable breaking the egg into the pan, feel free to break the egg into a cup to ensure you don't get any shell pieces mixed in, then pour the egg into the pocket. Repeat with the remaining eggs. Once all eggs have been placed into their pocket, pour water into the pan, cover with a lid, and let cook for about 3 minutes. Once the egg is firm and cooked, feel free to indulge. A good way to make sure the egg is cooked is to give the pan a little shake. If the egg appears jiggly, it may need another minute or two. If it is firm and doesn't show any motion when the pan is shaken, you're free to enjoy.

Prep time: 10 minutes

Cook time: 10 minutes

Cleanup time: 3 minutes

SERVES 2

Items needed: large sauté pan and lid, cutting board, chef knife, measuring device, and a wooden spoon

Optional item needed: small cup

29

LUNCH
RECIPES

TUNA BURGERS

Sometimes beef can get old, but eating a burger never will. While the space may be too tight in your fridge for burger meat, tuna can be stored in a cupboard for years. So when you're on the road for consecutive days, you can use your fridge space for other items besides beef, and avoid the inevitable bloody mess that it tends to leave behind.

- 2 5-ounce cans chunk tuna light, drained
- ¼ cup low-fat mayonnaise
- ½ cup breadcrumbs
- 1 tablespoon liquid eggs
- 2 tablespoons parsley, chopped
- 1 tablespoon Dijon mustard
- 1 teaspoon hot sauce
- 1 tablespoon coconut oil
- 2 large hamburger buns
- 1 beefsteak tomato

In a bowl, combine tuna, mayonnaise, breadcrumbs, parsley, mustard, and hot sauce. Mix well and form into 2½-inch-thick patties. Warm the oil in your cast-iron pan over medium heat. Once the pan is hot, lay the burgers down in it. Cook for 4 minutes, then flip the burger, turn the heat to low, and cook for 6 minutes. Serve on buns with a nice thick slice of tomato.

Prep time: 10 minutes   Stove time: 15 minutes

Cleanup time: 5 minutes

SERVES 2

Items needed: cast-iron pan, spatula, mixing bowl, measuring device, strainer, and can opener

CHICKEN CAESAR PASTA SALAD

This recipe puts the salad in pasta salad. Making sure you are eating enough greens is essential to staying healthy on the road. Eating just a salad can leave you hungry later on in the day, but adding a few carbohydrates and protein will fulfill your hunger needs and keep you energized.

- 2 cooked chicken breasts
- 12 ounces of cooked farfalle pasta
- 1 cup of your favorite Caesar dressing
- ½ cup parsley, chopped
- 1 cup frozen shelled edamame, thawed
- 1 head of romaine lettuce, chopped

Combine pasta, parsley, edamame, and dressing in a mixing bowl and mix thoroughly. Cut the chicken breast into ¼-inch-thick strips and add to the bowl with the romaine lettuce. Mix the ingredients in the bowl one more time, and then serve.

Prep time: 10 minutes

Cleanup time: 3 minutes

SERVES 2

Items needed: chef knife, cutting board, measuring cup, and mixing bowl

CRAB CAKES

Most Americans will never have the privilege of experiencing eating fresh crab. Fortunately, we have the luxury of canned crabmeat. It may not be ideal to eat it plain, but adding a few simple ingredients will be pleasantly surprising. Typically, canned crabmeat will list a drained weight ("dr. wt.") and a net weight ("net wt."); this recipe is based off of the drained weight, so plan accordingly.

- ⊃ 16 ounces drained fancy pink crabmeat
- ⊃ 1 stick of celery, finely chopped
- ⊃ ½ red bell pepper, finely chopped
- ⊃ ½ cup parsley, finely chopped
- ⊃ ½ cup liquid eggs
- ⊃ 1 teaspoon ground pepper
- ⊃ 1 tablespoon Tajín seasoning (typically found in the Hispanic seasoning section of your local grocery store)
- ⊃ ½ cup panko (breadcrumbs)
- ⊃ 1 teaspoon coconut oil

Thoroughly drain the crabmeat (preferably outside) and place in a mixing bowl with the panko, egg, pepper, and Tajín. In your cast-iron pan, heat the coconut oil over high heat, place the peppers and celery into the pan, and cook for 2 minutes. Place the cooked peppers and celery into the mixing bowl with the other ingredients and remove the pan from the heat. In the mixing bowl, thoroughly mix all of the ingredients and form 8 patties, 2 inches in diameter and ½ an inch thick. Return the pan to a medium heat and place the patties in the pan. Let cook for 4 minutes and then flip the cakes and continue cooking for 5 minutes. Remove the cakes from the pan and serve.

Prep time: 8 minutes   **Cook time:** 12 minutes   **Cleanup time:** 5 minutes

Items needed: mixing bowl, strainer, cast-iron pan, chef knife, metal spatula, and cutting board

TUNA SALAD

What I love about tuna salad is the diversity of what you can serve it on. You can put it on some bread for a tuna sandwich, or wrap it up in a piece of lettuce for a nice gluten-free option. My personal favorite, though, is to cut a nice thick slice of cucumber and put it right on top and enjoy. It's easy to make and doesn't require any cooking. It can be made with one bowl so the cleanup is quick and easy, which is why it is an essential recipe for your motorhome/ RV.

- 2 5-ounce cans of tuna, drained
- ½ cup celery, diced small
- 2 tablespoons low-fat mayonnaise
- 2 tablespoons parsley, chopped
- ½ cup relish
- 1 tablespoon Dijon mustard

Mix all the ingredients in a bowl and enjoy the freedom of choosing what to serve it on. Maybe you have some bread that needs to be used, or a couple of tortillas lying around. Have fun with it.

Prep time: 6 minutes

Cleanup time: 3 minutes

SERVES: 2

Items needed: can opener, cutting board, chef knife, measuring device, mixing bowl, and strainer

ULTIMATE PASTA SALAD

The list of pasta salads is practically endless. The recipe I provided requires minimal knife-work and is quick and easy. Pasta salads are a good way to get a substantial amount of nutrition in one bowl. It makes a perfect meal for those rest-area stops.

- 12 ounces cooked penne pasta
- 1 cup sun-dried tomatoes
- 1 cup artichoke hearts
- 1 cup roasted red peppers, sliced
- 8 Kalamata olives, halved
- ½ cup basil leaves, chopped
- ½ cup parsley, chopped
- 1 tablespoon olive oil

Place all of the ingredients in a bowl and mix well until the herbs coat all of the other ingredients evenly.

Prep time: 5 minutes

Cleanup time: 5 minutes

SERVES 2

Items needed: cutting board, chef knife, mixing bowl, and measuring device

SPRING ROLLS

Spring rolls are one of my favorite hands-on dishes to make. It is a very refreshing snack packed with a lot of flavor and is one of the healthiest recipes in this book. When cutting your vegetables, you want them to be the size of a toothpick (very thin). The hardest part about this recipe besides the knife skills required is rolling the rice paper tightly enough without having it rip; it's very similar to rolling a burrito. Spring-roll wrappers (rice paper) are usually found in the Asian cuisine section of your grocery store.

- 4 spring-roll wrappers
- 2 cups Napa cabbage, thinly sliced
- 2 cups cucumber, peeled and thinly sliced
- 2 cups carrots, shredded
- 8 long green onions
- 2 avocados, pitted and cut thin
- 2 tablespoons cilantro leaves, chopped
- 2 tablespoons soy sauce
- 1 teaspoon sriracha

Lay out 2 dinner plates and cover the bottom of one plate with warm water. Dip the spring-roll wrapper into the water until it's fully submerged for 5 seconds, then transfer to the dry plate and let sit for 1 minute. Evenly disperse a ½ cup each of Napa cabbage, cucumber, carrots, and avocado, 1 tablespoon of cilantro, and 2 green onions in a line just off the center of your wrapper, leaving 2 inches of wrapper on each side of your vegetables. Fold the sides over the top of the vegetables, roll the shorter flap over them, and continue to roll tightly so the veggies are firm and tight inside the wrap. Repeat until all ingredients and wraps have been used. In a small bowl, combine soy sauce and sriracha and use for dipping sauce.

Prep time: 15 minutes

Cleanup time: 5 minutes

SERVES 2

Items needed: 2 deep dinner plates, measuring device, cutting board, and chef knife

43

HAWAIIAN BARBECUE (LUAU) SLIDERS

I love the Hawaiian culture, especially luaus. The main ingredients for a proper luau are pork, pineapple, and barbecue sauce. I've created a recipe that involves all of those ingredients, so you're basically having a motorhome/RV luau! When cooking the pork, you have several options. If you're in a hurry, you can buy thin-cut pork tenderloin and cook them in your cast-iron pan. If you have time to spare, it's worth it to buy a whole pork tenderloin and roast it in your oven at 350°F for 25 minutes. Make sure it's cooked to 160°F before consuming. So put on those Hawaiian shirts, turn on some Hawaiian music, and enjoy!

- ⊃ 6 King's Hawaiian rolls
- ⊃ 6 thin slices of pork tenderloin
- ⊃ 6 pineapple chunks
- ⊃ 6 tablespoons barbecue sauce
- ⊃ Pinch salt and pepper

Season each side of the pork tenderloin with salt and pepper. Heat your cast-iron pan over high heat. Lay the pork in the pan and dry-sear on one side for 5 minutes. Turn heat to low and flip the pork. Continue cooking for 8 minutes until pork is cooked through. Place the pineapple in the pan, let cook for 1 minute, and then turn off the heat. Pour 1 tablespoon of barbecue sauce on each slice of pork and let it sit in the pan for 1 minute. Open the buns and place 1 slice of pork on each bun and top with the pineapple.

Prep time: 5 minutes   Cook time: 15 minutes   Cleanup time: 5 minutes

SERVES 2

Items needed: cast-iron pan, knife, and cutting board

CANAPÉS, HORS D'OEUVRES, SNACKS AND MUNCHIES

BOATMAN'S DELIGHT

Although road-tripping has nothing to do with boating, this recipe earned its name by offering a delightful snack for hungry boatmen who need a quick bite to help them power through the day. Being a captain of a motorhome/RV can be just as exhausting and draining as spending a day on the water. This is a great snack to make in advance and always have in your fridge simply because its shelf life is about two weeks, it spreads real nicely on a tortilla, and it packs you with carbohydrates that are needed to power through the rest of the day. For a healthier version, substitute spreadable goat cheese for the cream cheese.

- 8 ounces cream cheese, softened
- 4 ounces sliced olives, drained
- ½ red onion, diced small
- ½ cup dill, chopped
- Tortilla or pita bread

Once cream cheese has softened, add it to a mixing bowl with the olives, onions, and dill. Mix thoroughly until all of the ingredients are incorporated evenly throughout the cream cheese. Feel free to spread it on a tortilla or a piece of pita bread—your preference.

Prep time: 5 minutes

Cleanup time: 5 minutes

SERVES 2

Items needed: cutting board, chef knife, measuring device, mixing bowl, and wooden spoon

BLACK BEAN AND CORN SALSA

This salsa really captures the Southwestern feel. If you're traveling through Utah, Arizona, Texas, New Mexico, or even southern Colorado, this recipe will fit right in. If spicy food isn't really your thing, just skip adding the jalapeños.

- 1 can sweet corn, strained
- 1 can seasoned black beans, strained
- 3 Roma tomatoes, diced small
- 1 white onion, diced small
- 3 tablespoons cilantro, chopped
- 3 jalapeños, diced small
- 5 tablespoons lime juice
- 1 tablespoon salt
- 1 teaspoon pepper

Mix all ingredients together in a mixing bowl and serve with your favorite tortilla chip.

Prep time: 10 minutes

Cleanup time: 5 minutes

SERVES 3

Items needed: mixing bowl, strainer, can opener, cutting board, chef knife, and measuring device

QUINOA TABBOULEH

Tabbouleh has been a staple recipe with my family since I can remember, and it still remains on the top of my list as a favorite. It offers a nice, refreshing, zesty taste with mint and citrus. This is a perfect lunchtime meal to put on a pita or tortilla with a little goat or cream cheese smeared on it.

- ➲ 2 cups cooled, cooked quinoa
- ➲ ½ cup mint, chopped
- ➲ ½ cup parsley leaves
- ➲ ¼ cup chives, chopped
- ➲ 10 cherry tomatoes, halved
- ➲ ½ cup sliced olives
- ➲ 3 tablespoons lemon juice
- ➲ 1 tablespoon olive oil
- ➲ 1 cup crumbled feta, cream cheese, or goat cheese (optional)
- ➲ 2 pita breads or tortillas (optional)

Combine all of the ingredients in a bowl and mix thoroughly. Serving on a pita or a tortilla with feta, goat, or cream cheese really complements the tabbouleh and helps cut out some of the unwanted quinoa flavor.

Prep time: 8 minutes

Cleanup time: 5 minutes

SERVES 2

Items needed: mixing bowl, chef knife, cutting board, and measuring device

BEAN AND QUINOA SALAD

Packed with protein and fiber, this recipe is designed to keep your energy levels high to help you power through the long days on the road. Edamame is best stored in your freezer but can thaw fairly quickly. Feel free to mix frozen edamame into the bowl with the other ingredients; just be sure to wait about ten minutes to let the edamame thaw to a tender but crunchy texture. Enjoying this recipe in a leaf of iceberg lettuce makes for a fun dining experience.

- 2 cups cooked quinoa
- 1 can seasoned black beans, drained
- 2 cups frozen shelled edamame, thawed
- ½ cup green onions
- 12 cherry tomatoes, halved
- 2 tablespoons cilantro, chopped
- 3 tablespoons lemon juice
- 1 head of iceberg lettuce (optional)

Combine all of the ingredients in a bowl (except optional iceberg lettuce) and mix well. Pull off a leaf of lettuce and spoon the salad into the cup it forms. Eat it like you would a taco.

Prep time: 5 minutes

Cleanup time: 2 minutes

SERVES 3

Items needed: mixing bowl, chef knife, cutting board, and measuring device

GRAND CANYON CUCUMBERS

While traveling long distances, stops can be short and rare. There may be times where you have to prep a snack in a matter of minutes, on minimal space, using minimal dishes. If there is one snack that has stuck with me throughout the years that has kept the joy of snacking alive and fresh, this is the one, named after a 25-day trip down the Grand Canyon, when supplies were depleted and the food selection was minimal. These three ingredients presented themselves in a magical way to make us say, "Wow, that's pretty good!"

- ⊃ 1 cucumber
- ⊃ 2 tablespoons lime juice
- ⊃ 2 tablespoons Tajín seasoning

Slice cucumber in 1/8-inch-thick slices and lay them on a dinner plate. Pour the lime juice evenly over the cucumbers. Then distribute the Tajín over the cucumbers. Doesn't get any easier.

Prep time: 3 minutes

Cleanup time: 1 minute

SERVES 2

Items needed: cutting board, chef knife, and dinner plate

GUACAMOLE

The healthiest of all the dips, guacamole can be very beneficial for your nutritional intake while traveling to foreign lands. It's a heart-healthy snack that can lower cholesterol and is packed with fiber. While I could personally eat an avocado by itself, it goes great with the following ingredients, mixed in a bowl and used as a dip, topping, or incorporated into a burrito or omelet.

- 3 ripe avocados
- 1 small red onion, finely diced
- 1 Roma tomato, diced small
- 1 tablespoon cilantro, chopped
- 1 tablespoon lime juice
- Pinch of salt and pepper

Clean the avocados by removing the pits and peels, then place into a bowl with the tomato, onion, cilantro, lime juice, and salt and pepper. Using a fork, combine the ingredients and press until everything is mixed thoroughly.

Prep time: 10 minutes

Cleanup time: 5 minutes

SERVES 2

Items needed: cutting board, chef knife, large spoon, measuring device, and mixing bowl

PICO DE GALLO

One of the best parts about eating out at a Mexican restaurant is the chips and salsa at the beginning of the meal. Now you can bring that same Mexican atmosphere that you might find south of the border to your motorhome/RV. This is a perfect afternoon snack to put on the table with your favorite tortilla chip and have a mini fiesta.

- ⊃ 8 Roma tomatoes, diced small
- ⊃ 2 jalapeños, diced small
- ⊃ 1 small red onion, diced small
- ⊃ 2 tablespoons cilantro, chopped
- ⊃ 3 tablespoons lime juice
- ⊃ 1 bag of your favorite tortilla chips

Mix all of your ingredients into a bowl and serve with your choice of chips.

Prep time: 10 minutes

Cleanup time: 3 minutes

SERVES 2

Items needed: cutting board, chef knife, and mixing bowl

Optional items: cerveza and tequila

THE PINWHEEL

A quick snack that requires no cooking time is essential for life on the road with a condensed kitchen. The pinwheel is basically cream cheese tightly rolled up in a tortilla, then cut into ½-inch slices. The recipe that I chose for this book is a healthy version using goat cheese. Goat cheese has 3 times more protein, with fewer carbohydrates and less fat. Adding the other ingredients gives it a nice Southwestern taste.

- ⮂ 1 cup roasted red peppers, diced
- ⮂ 1 cup canned black beans, drained
- ⮂ 2 tablespoons cilantro, chopped
- ⮂ 12 ounces spreadable goat cheese
- ⮂ 2 large tortillas

Distribute all ingredients evenly over both tortillas. Roll the tortillas tightly and cut into ½-inch-thick slices.

Prep time: 5 minutes

Cleanup time: 2 minutes

SERVES 2

Items needed: chef knife, cutting board, strainer, and measuring device

TRAIL MIX

What's nice about making trail mix in advance is that you get to enjoy all of your favorite products in one bite, instead of having 5 open bags of product that will end up going stale by the time you get back around to them. The Smartfood White Cheddar Popcorn is one of the key ingredients because when you mix it in a bag with all of the other products, it shares some of that delicious seasoning with the other ingredients, like the pretzels and nuts. I believe you will find the benefit of making your own trail mix within the first bite.

- 10 ounces Snyder's Mini Pretzels
- 8 ounces Planters cashews
- 6.25 ounces Planters macadamias
- 6.3 ounces Goldfish, regular
- 5 ounces Smartfood White Cheddar Popcorn
- 2 3.14-ounce bags of milk chocolate M&M's
- 1-gallon ziplock bag

Start by pouring the bag of pretzels into the ziplock bag first, so that they sit at the bottom and gather the seasoning that falls off of the other products. The next product to pour into the bag is the Goldfish. After that, pour in the popcorn so it creates a barrier for the smaller items and will prevent them from falling to the bottom and picking up an unwanted flavor. Finally, pour in the nuts and M&M's. When you're ready to indulge, give your ziplock bag a nice shake so everything is mixed to your liking.

DINNER
RECIPES

MAC AND CHEESE

Although the pasta used in this dish isn't macaroni, farfalle (aka bow-tie pasta) is more suitable for this dish because it doesn't have any hollow spots that ingredients can get stuck in and not cook properly. Also, feel free to substitute the edamame with fine-cut broccoli, green beans, or any other type of vegetable you may have lying around.

- ⊃ 2 cups of heavy cream
- ⊃ 12 ounces cooked farfalle pasta
- ⊃ 1 cup ham steak, diced small
- ⊃ 6 ounces finely shredded mild cheddar cheese
- ⊃ 1 cup frozen shelled edamame
- ⊃ 2 tablespoons parsley, chopped
- ⊃ 1 tablespoon salt
- ⊃ 1 teaspoon ground pepper

In a large saucepot, bring your cream to a boil. Let the cream boil for 3 minutes while it reduces and thickens (keeping an eye on the boiling cream, as it tends to boil over the pot, causing an unwanted mess). After 3 minutes of boiling, pour in the pasta with the edamame and ham, and let cook for 2 more minutes. Pour in the cheese, salt, pepper, and parsley, and then remove from heat. Stir until the cheese has melted and a sauce has formed. Don't let the sauce boil, as that tends to give it a grainy texture.

Prep time: 5 minutes

Cook time: 12 minutes

Cleanup time: 5 minutes

SERVES 2

Items needed: large saucepot, measuring device, wooden spoon, chef knife, and cutting board

MARGHERITA POLENTA PIZZA

Did you ever think that you would be making pizza in your motorhome? It may not be your traditional pizza, but it just might be your new favorite. This recipe gives you the joy of pizza without the hassle of having to mess with yeast and the whole process of making dough. It provides that fresh-baked taste you miss out on with frozen pizzas. Margherita pizza has always been my favorite, but feel free to use your own ingredients. If polenta is not available at the store, feel free to use yellow cornmeal; it's a perfect substitute.

- ⊃ 1 cup fine polenta
- ⊃ ½ cup all-purpose flour
- ⊃ 1 teaspoon baking powder
- ⊃ ¼ cup liquid eggs
- ⊃ ⅔ cup milk
- ⊃ ½ cup grated Parmesan
- ⊃ ½ cup marinara sauce
- ⊃ 4 ounces grated mozzarella
- ⊃ 1 Roma tomato, diced
- ⊃ 2 tablespoons basil, chopped
- ⊃ 1 tablespoon coconut oil

Preheat oven to 375°F. In a bowl, mix together the polenta, flour, and baking powder. Pour in the egg and milk and mix until a thick batter has formed, then finish with Parmesan and gently mix. Heat your cast-iron pan over a medium heat with the coconut oil, until the oil coats the bottom of the pan. Add the polenta batter to the pan, spread evenly onto the bottom of the pan, and cook over the medium heat until the base has set (about 4 minutes). Spread the marinara over the top of the crust and add mozzarella and tomatoes. Place the pan into the oven and bake for 12 minutes until cheese is melted and crust is lightly browned. Remove from oven and let cool.

Prep time: 6 minutes

Cook time: 20 minutes

Cleanup time: 8 minutes

SERVES 3

Items needed: mixing bowl, cast-iron pan, measuring device, and chef knife

SALMON BURGERS

While canned salmon isn't as appealing as other forms of salmon, you will be pleasantly surprised with the flavor and nutrition this recipe offers you. Because most of the ingredients can easily be stowed in your cupboards, it will save room in your fridge for more important items, and will prevent you from running your fridge the entire trip.

- 2 5-ounce cans of skinless, boneless salmon, drained
- ½ cup panko (breadcrumbs)
- 1 tablespoon low-fat mayonnaise
- ¼ cup carrots, grated
- 1 tablespoon ginger powder
- 2 tablespoons green onion, chopped
- ¼ cup liquid eggs
- 1 tablespoon cilantro
- 1 tablespoon soy sauce
- 1 tablespoon coconut oil
- 2 hamburger buns
- 2 slices of beefsteak tomato (optional)
- 2 leaves of lettuce (optional)

Drain the salmon and combine in a mixing bowl with the panko, mayonnaise, carrots, ginger powder, green onions, liquid eggs, cilantro, and soy sauce. Mix well until panko is thoroughly absorbed. Form your patties to the size of your bun, about a ½ inch thick. Heat your cast-iron pan over medium heat and add the oil. Once the coconut oil is heated, place your salmon patties into the pan and cook the patties for 5 minutes, then flip, turn your heat down to low, and continue cooking for another 6 minutes. Serve on a bun with a tomato slice and a piece of lettuce.

Prep time: 10 minutes

Cook time: 12 minutes

Cleanup time: 5 minutes

SERVES 2

Items needed: cast-iron pan, mixing bowl, cutting board, chef knife, measuring device, can opener, strainer, and spatula

SHRIMP AND RISOTTO

This recipe is one of the more difficult ones, but I believe it will be well worth your while. It's the perfect meal to go with that bottle of wine you might have picked up at a vineyard along your travels. If risotto isn't available at the store, you can substitute Arborio rice. Also, when selecting your Parmesan, the better quality it is, the better quality your dish will be.

RISOTTO

- ½ cup risotto
- ½ small white onion, chopped
- 1 tablespoon garlic, chopped fine
- 2 tablespoon chives, chopped
- 2 cups chicken broth
- ½ cup water
- 1 tablespoon white wine
- 1 tablespoon salt
- ½ cup of grated Parmigiano-Reggiano (genuine Parmesan)
- 2 tablespoons canola oil

In a large pot, warm your canola oil over medium heat and add your risotto, onion, and garlic. Stirring frequently with a wooden spoon or rubber spatula, cook until onions appear translucent and garlic starts to brown (about 2 minutes). Then add your white wine and cook until all the wine has evaporated (about 1 minute). Leaving your pot on medium heat, add your salt, and water; then add your chicken broth by pouring it in a quarter cup at a time. Stirring frequently, let cook until the risotto becomes exposed and most of the liquid has evaporated (about 10 minutes) and remove from heat. Finally, add your Parmesan with the chives and stir well.

SHRIMP

- 12 large peeled shrimp
- 1 tablespoon cumin
- 1 tablespoon coconut oil

In a cast-iron, heat your coconut oil over a medium heat until melted. Lay out the shrimp on your cutting board and season each side of the shrimp with cumin. Place them in the heated pan and cook on each side until the shrimp becomes solid white and firm (about 5 minutes per side).

Prep time: 5 minutes
Cook time: 20 minutes
Cleanup time: 5 minutes

SERVES 2

Items needed: large saucepot, large skillet, measuring device, wooden spoon, chef knife, and cutting board

STEAK FAJITAS

I prefer to have fajitas rather than tacos in my motorhome simply because there is less preparation involved. Also because fajitas have more flavor than tacos. If you've ever been sitting and waiting for your dinner at an authentic Mexican restaurant and all of the sudden you hear this sizzling skillet coming out of the kitchen and all eyes are focused on this dish that sounds like a Fourth of July celebration, well, this is that dish.

- ⮑ 1 pound beef sirloin steak, cut into thin strips
- ⮑ 1 bell pepper, thinly sliced
- ⮑ 1 white onion, thinly sliced
- ⮑ 6 ounces shredded cheddar cheese
- ⮑ ½ cup sour cream
- ⮑ 6 flour tortillas
- ⮑ 1 tablespoon olive oil
- ⮑ 1 tablespoon coconut oil
- ⮑ 1 tablespoon cumin
- ⮑ 1 tablespoon sriracha
- ⮑ 1 tablespoon salt
- ⮑ 1 teaspoon pepper

In a mixing bowl, combine steak, olive oil, cumin, salt, pepper, and sriracha. Heat coconut oil in your cast-iron pan over medium heat. Once pan is hot, place the meat in the pan and let it cook. Stir frequently until the steak has browned (about 3 minutes). Toss the veggies in the same bowl the steak was in so they can absorb any seasoning that may be left. Place the veggies in the pan and cook for 5 minutes while stirring frequently, then kill the heat. To warm the tortillas, lay them on top of the ingredients so that each tortilla is exposed to the steam and let sit for about 3 minutes. Use the sour cream and shredded cheddar as condiments to place on top of your assembled fajita.

Prep time: 12 minutes

Cook time: 15 minutes

Cleanup time: 6 minutes

SERVES 2

Items needed: cast-iron pan, mixing bowl, cutting board, chef knife, measuring device, tongs, and wooden spoon

STIR-FRY

The variety of stir-fry noodles is vast; feel free to explore all of the types that are offered. Some of the most common stir-fry noodles are udon, cellophane, rice, ramen, and soba noodles. While any of these will work in this recipe, I prefer lo-mein noodles, simply because the cooking process is fast and easy. Make sure to follow the directions provided on the package of noodles that you decide on.

STIR-FRY

- ➲ 2 skinless chicken breasts, cut into ½-inch strips
- ➲ 1 package cooked stir-fry noodles
- ➲ 1 red bell pepper, cut into 1-inch cubes
- ➲ 1 cup carrots, thinly sliced
- ➲ 1 white onion, thinly sliced
- ➲ 1 cup frozen shelled edamame, thawed
- ➲ 2 tablespoons garlic
- ➲ 2 tablespoons canola oil

Heat your sauté pan on medium heat and add 1 tablespoon of oil. Once the oil is hot, add the chicken and cook thoroughly (about 7 minutes). Once the chicken is cooked, add carrots, bell pepper, and onion to the pan and cook for about 2 minutes. Turn the heat to low and add the edamame and garlic. Cook for 1 minute, and then add the sauce.

STIR-FRY SAUCE

- ➲ ¾ cup of broth (veggie, beef, or chicken)
- ➲ ¼ cup Mae Ploy sweet chili sauce
- ➲ ¼ cup soy sauce

To avoid dirtying another pan, feel free to pour the broth, soy sauce, and Mae Ploy sauce straight into the pan and stir well. Place the noodles on the very top and let the steam from the pan warm the stir-fry noodles. After about a minute, go ahead and stir all of the ingredients in the pan together. Once the sauce has been mixed in and coats all of the ingredients, go ahead and serve.

Prep time: 10 minutes

Cook time: 20 minutes

Cleanup time: 8 minutes

SERVES 3

Items needed: sauté pan, cutting board, chef knife, and measuring device

MAE PLOY-GLAZED TILAPIA WITH BASMATI HERB RICE

Basmati rice is a delicate rice that cooks more easily and quickly than any other rice, which makes it essential for cooking in your motorhome. Similarly, since most tilapia is cut thin, it makes for a quick bake time, so you won't have to use a lot of propane to cook it. Mae Ploy sauce is a delicious sweet sauce that is usually found in the Asian sauce section of your local grocery store.

BASMATI HERB RICE

- ➲ 2 cups water
- ➲ 1 cup basmati rice
- ➲ 1 tablespoon cilantro, finely chopped
- ➲ 1 tablespoon chives, finely chopped
- ➲ 1 tablespoon dill, finely chopped
- ➲ 1 tablespoon unsalted butter, softened
- ➲ 1 tablespoon salt
- ➲ 1 teaspoon coconut oil

Combine the water, rice, oil, and salt in a pot and bring to a boil, then reduce the heat to low and cover. Let cook for about 5 to 7 minutes, checking frequently to make sure all water is evaporating. Once the water has evaporated, transfer to a mixing bowl and add the butter and herbs. Gently fold the rice with the herbs and butter until all ingredients are mixed evenly.

MAE PLOY-GLAZED TILAPIA

2 6-ounce thinly sliced portions of tilapia

4 tablespoons Mae Ploy sweet chili sauce

Preheat oven to 350°F. Spray a baking sheet with non-stick spray, place your tilapia in the center, and cook for about 10 minutes. Pull out the fish and evenly coat each piece of tilapia with the Mae Ploy sauce, then finish cooking for about 2 minutes. Once fish is cooked all the way through, serve with the rice.

Prep time: 5 minutes

Cook time: 15 minutes

Cleanup time: 5 minutes

SERVES 2

Items needed: saucepot with lid, baking sheet, cutting board, chef knife, measuring device, and mixing bowl

WARM PENNE WITH HAM, EDAMAME, AND OREGANO

This pasta dish is quick and easy for the nights that may be spent boondocking in a parking lot while traveling. It's quick and easy, with a nice taste of herb and garlic, and will supply you with the carbohydrates to give you the energy to get back on the road bright and early the next day.

- 12 ounces cooked penne pasta
- 1 cup frozen shelled edamame
- 1 tablespoon coconut oil
- 2 cups diced ham steak
- 2 cloves garlic, chopped
- 2 tablespoons dried oregano
- 1 tablespoon salt
- 1 tablespoon butter
- ¼ cup water
- Handful of arugula (optional)

In a sauté pan, warm the coconut oil over medium heat and add garlic, ham, and edamame. Cook until the edamame is warm and thawed. Add the pasta, salt, and water to the pan and cover. Turn heat to low and cook until water is evaporated. Finish with the oregano and butter. If desired or available, throw in a handful of arugula to add some more nutrition and a little peppery taste.

Prep time: 5 minutes   **Cook time:** 10 minutes   **Cleanup:** 5 minutes

SERVES 2

Items needed: sauté pan, cutting board, chef knife, and measuring device

CHICKEN RAMEN BOWL

Have you ever cooked Asian cuisine? If not, let this be your first. And if you have, you may have found your new favorite recipe. Instead of using artificial flavoring packets that are extremely high in sodium and very bland, you'll find that this broth recipe is sweet and spicy and will provide you with more nutrition than the factory seasoning packets offer. This recipe is keen for those chilly nights that may be spent in the higher elevations in the colder seasons of the year.

- ➲ 2 thin skinless chicken breasts
- ➲ 2 3.5-ounce packages of ramen noodles
- ➲ 2 eggs
- ➲ 2 tablespoons soy sauce
- ➲ 2 carrots, thin sliced
- ➲ ½ cup chives, sliced
- ➲ 4 cups chicken broth
- ➲ ½ cup Mae Ploy sweet chili sauce
- ➲ 1 tablespoon sriracha

In a large saucepot, bring the chicken broth, Mae Ploy sauce, soy sauce, and sriracha to a boil. Place the chicken breast and 2 whole eggs into the pot and boil for 10 minutes. Remove the chicken and the eggs from the pot, peel the eggs, and cut the chicken into thin strips and set aside (caution: may be hot). Place the ramen noodles in the pot and cook for 2 minutes. Place the chicken, carrots, and chives into the pot with the noodles and cook for 3 more minutes. Evenly distribute the contents of the pot between 2 bowls and top with the peeled, halved eggs.

Prep time: 5 minutes   Cook time: 18 minutes   Cleanup time: 5 minutes

SERVES 2

Items needed: large saucepot, cutting board, chef knife, and measuring device

DESSERT
RECIPES

BERRY CRUMBLE

Getting a daily serving of fruits can be very important while traveling, especially when it can easily be skipped while not being exposed to fruits at gas stations or rest areas. This dish provides you with the sweet taste of dessert and your daily serving of berries.

CRUMBLE TOPPING

- ¾ cup almonds, crushed
- ⅓ cup quick-cooking oats
- 2 teaspoons sugar
- 1 teaspoon nutmeg
- 1 teaspoon cinnamon
- 2 tablespoons butter, softened

Combine almonds, oats, sugar, cinnamon, and nutmeg in a bowl. Using a fork, mix ingredients, then add butter and firmly press until you have large coarse crumbs. Transfer crumble to another dish so you can strain the berry juice into the bowl.

BERRY FILLING

- 20 ounces frozen mixed berries, thawed
- 1 teaspoon sugar
- 1 teaspoon cornstarch

Preheat oven to 375°F. Strain the berry liquid into a bowl, and add the cornstarch and sugar to the juice. Place the strained berries in your cast-iron pan, and pour your berry liquid over the top. Disperse your crumble mixture evenly over the top, and then place into the heated oven for about 20 minutes, until berries are bubbly. Pull out and let cool.

Prep time: 10 minutes

Cook time: 20 minutes

Cleanup time: 8 minutes

SERVES 3

Items needed: mixing bowl, strainer, cast-iron pan, measuring device, and fork

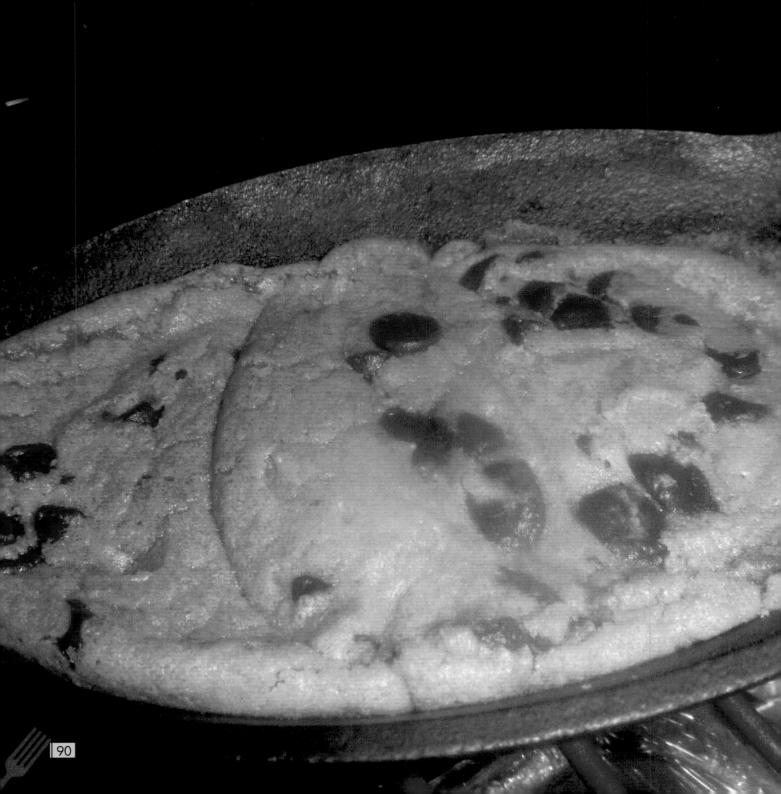

CAST-IRON COOKIE BAKE

It may be easier just to buy your favorite kind of cookie in the grocery store and save yourself the time and fuss of dealing with baking, but maybe you're celebrating a birthday on the road, or it's your anniversary, or you want to show off the commodities of your motorhome. Then let the baking begin! Fresh-baked cookies; there's nothing like it. This recipe goes great with a scoop of ice cream right on top.

- 6 tablespoons unsalted butter, softened
- 1 cup all-purpose flour
- 1/3 cup brown sugar
- ½ cup granulated sugar
- ¼ cup liquid eggs
- 1 teaspoon vanilla extract
- ½ teaspoon baking soda
- 1 cup chocolate chips

Preheat the oven to 350°F. In a large mixing bowl, combine butter and both sugars. With a wooden spoon, fold ingredients together until creamy. Add the egg, vanilla, flour, and baking soda, and mix thoroughly. Add the chocolate chips at the end and mix into the dough gently. Spray your cast-iron pan with a non-stick spray and press the dough into the pan so there is a nice even layer. Place in your heated oven and let bake for 20 minutes. Pull and let cool, then cut like a pie. Now your motorhome will have the inviting aroma of fresh-baked cookies. Hope you're hungry!

Prep time: 5 minutes   Cook time: 20 minutes   Cleanup time: 5 minutes

SERVES 4

Items needed: mixing bowl, measuring device, small cast-iron pan, and wooden spoon

CHERRY PARFAIT WITH CANDIED NUTS

While the parfait is one of the easier desserts to make, its layered flavors can make you appear to be a top chef. It also gives you a chance to explore your culinary art skills. Using different flavored fillings and toppings can let you make your cup a colorful delight. This recipe is one of my favorites simply because of the crunch that the nuts present, and because the frozen yogurt can cool you down on those warm nights. Don't feel like you're limited to eat this in the evening; it can be a great snack for the long open road when you want something cool and sweet.

- ⊃ 1 cup cherry pie filling
- ⊃ 1 cup vanilla frozen yogurt
- ⊃ 1 cup low-fat Redi-Whip
- ⊃ ½ cup candied nuts (your choice)

Lay out two parfait glasses and spoon 2 tablespoons of frozen yogurt into each of the glasses. On top of that, place 2 tablespoons of the cherry pie filling. Repeat twice and finish with Redi-Whip and candied nuts.

Prep time: 5 minutes

Cleanup time: 5 minutes

SERVES 2

Items needed: ice cream scoop, parfait glasses, and measuring device

CHOCOLATE-Y S'MORES BARS

Much of my childhood consisted of sitting around a campfire perfecting my marshmallow-roasting technique. While some people preferred them crispy black, I always took pride in getting mine golden brown. All in all, that was the taste of camping for me: a nice s'mores eaten on a stump, with only the campfire as my light. While everyone (hopefully) knows how to make a s'more, I wanted to bring that same taste to a dish that can be enjoyed without having to worry about building a fire or finding a campsite that even allows fires.

- ⊃ ¼ cup butter, cubed
- ⊃ 1 10-ounce package of marshmallows
- ⊃ 1 12-ounce package Golden Graham Cereal
- ⊃ 1/3 cup milk chocolate chips

In a large sauté pan, melt butter over low heat. Once melted, add the marshmallows and cook until they're well blended and soft, about 2 minutes. Remove from the heat and stir the Golden Grahams into the mixture. Pour the mixture into the pan and use a spatula to press evenly into a greased 13-by-9-inch pan. Distribute the chocolate chips evenly on top and place in fridge until completely cool. Cut into bars and store what is left in an airtight container.

SERVES: 6

Prep time: 5 minutes

Cook time: 8 minutes

Cleanup time: 5 minutes

Items needed: 13-by-9-inch oven-safe pan, large sauté pan, spatula, and measuring device

KEY LIME PIE

This Key lime pie recipe is one of the easiest and cheapest to make. The most important step is to make sure the pie has enough time to set. And since it yields about 6 servings, you can eat it for more than one night. The longer it sits in the freezer, the firmer it becomes.

- 8-ounce tub of low-fat whipped cream
- 14-ounce can low-fat sweetened condensed milk
- ½ cup lime juice
- 6-ounce graham-cracker pie crust

Mix the whipped cream, sweetened condensed milk, and lime juice in a bowl, and blend until smooth. Transfer the mixture into the pie crust, and place in freezer for about 30 minutes, until it has set and is firm. Store leftovers in the freezer.

Prep time: 5 minutes

Freeze time: 30 minutes

Cleanup time: 5 minutes

SERVES 6

Items needed: mixing bowl, whisk, and measuring device

POUND CAKE WITH ALMOND CREAM

Pound cake is one of the most durable cakes to travel with. It can survive most of the elements that you will encounter on the road; whether it's the dry desert heat or below-freezing temperatures, pound cake can hold up. It's also easy to combine with other ingredients to give your dessert layers of flavor.

- ⮑ ¼ cup slivered almonds
- ⮑ 4 1-inch slices of pound cake
- ⮑ 2 cups low- fat whipped cream
- ⮑ ½ tablespoon almond extract
- ⮑ ½ teaspoon vanilla extract

Place the almonds in a dry skillet over medium heat and toast until golden brown (about 3 minutes), frequently shaking the pan to prevent your nuts from burning.

In a bowl, mix the whipped topping with almond and vanilla extract. Spoon this mixture over the pound cake and top with your toasted almonds.

Cook time: 5 minutes

Prep time: 5 minutes

Cleanup time: 3 minutes

SERVES 2

Items needed: sauté pan, mixing bowl, measuring device, and chef knife

PUDDING-FILLED SPONGE CAKES WITH FRESH BERRIES

Having a dessert that requires no oven time or fridge space will save you from having to use your propane, and the hassle of finding a hook-up. Simple desserts like this were designed for the nights spent boondocking in parking lots or rest areas. Feel free to use your favorite flavor of pudding and not just vanilla.

- ➲ 2 cups of fresh berries (your choice)
- ➲ 1 tablespoon lemon juice
- ➲ 2 teaspoons granulated sugar
- ➲ 4 mini sponge cakes
- ➲ 2 vanilla pudding packs

Gently mix the berries, lemon juice, and sugar in a mixing bowl. Distribute the pudding evenly over the sponge cakes, and then top with the berry mixture. It's that easy, which makes it taste even sweeter.

Prep time: 5 minutes

Cleanup time: 2 minutes

SERVES 2

Items needed: mixing bowl, and measuring device

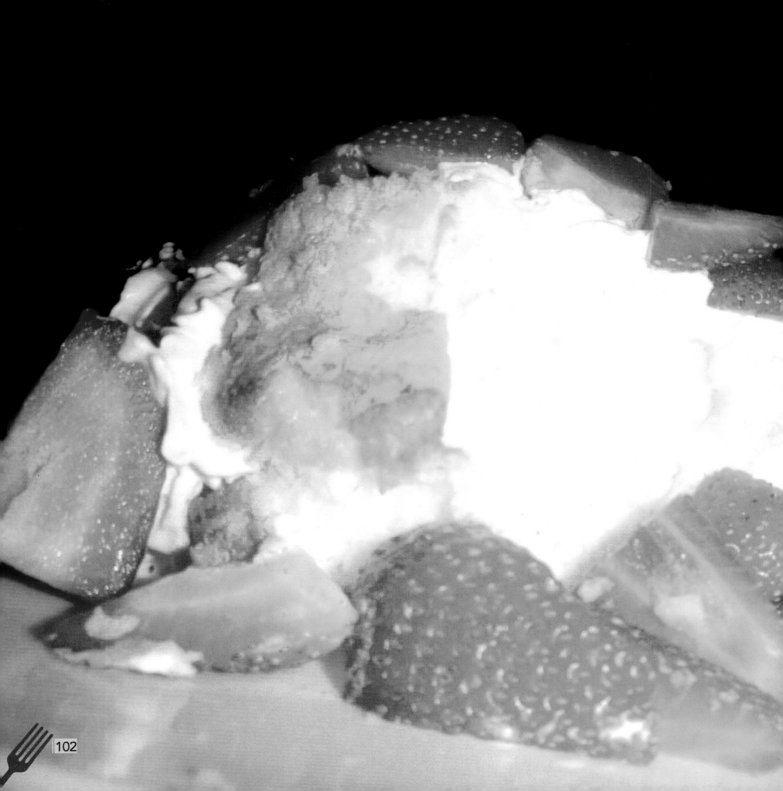

STRAWBERRIES AND CREAM ON ANGEL FOOD CAKE

Traveling across the country tends to be a little overwhelming at times; that's why it's nice to have a dessert recipe that is quick and easy and can really take the edge off of those long days on the road. Angel food cake is always easy to find and is typically a low-priced dessert. This recipe may seem like a no-brainer, but when you're traveling, the last thing on your mind is an easy dessert recipe. This book is here to remind you of just how easy it can be.

- ➲ 2 slices of angel food cake
- ➲ 4 ounces low-fat Redi-Whip
- ➲ 8 strawberries, sliced

Place a slice of angel food cake into each bowl, and disperse 2 ounces of whipped cream onto each slice. Finish by topping each slice with 4 berries.

Prep time: 5 minutes

Cleanup time: 3 minutes

SERVES 2

ABOUT THE AUTHOR

Most of my childhood was spent camping out on the river or in the woods. I became very keen on preparing meals for overnight trips. One of my fondest memories was my family loading up the motorhome for the Fourth of July weekend and hitting the road. It was then that I knew I wanted my life to involve owning a motorhome. Since that has become a reality I found my enthusiasm for cooking and preparing meals in my motorhome. Cooking has always come naturally to me. I began cooking professionally at the age of 18 and have since been cooking for the rich and famous in Aspen, amassing a vast number of recipes and menus along the way. I've made spaetzel for Arnold Schwarzenegger, tossed a salad for Uma Thurman, and nourished famous celebrities like Robert de Niro and Will Ferrell.

While conversing with other motorhome/RVers, I've discovered the majority of them prefer to cook out of their own kitchens rather than dining out. It was then that I decided I wanted to share my knowledge and recipes with the world of motorhomers. I wanted to create recipes that are quick, easy, and nourishing so that planning meals could be done with ease. I wanted to share the fulfillment of creating meals that are delicious and rewarding. My passion for cooking has created this book for you and your crew to enjoy these delicious recipes on the road.

My hope is that this book will spark a passion for cooking and planning your own meals, while letting you enjoy your vacation or life on the road. I too love to dine out and see what restaurants in the area have to offer, but most of the time I'm looking for a quick, easy meal that won't consume all of my day. Other times I'll be at a rest area looking for a bite to eat, and that is where these recipes were created.